What's So Great About Chopin?

A Biography of Frederic Chopin Just for Kids!

Sam Rogers

KidLit-O Books
www.kidlito.com

© 2014. All Rights Reserved.

Cover Image © majo - Fotolia.com

Table of Contents

ABOUT KIDCAPS 3

INTRODUCTION 4

CHAPTER 1: EARLY CHILDHOOD............................6

CHAPTER 2: RISE OF THE MUSICAL PRODIGY..**15**

CHAPTER 3: CHOPIN, THE ROMANTIC **28**

CHAPTER 4: REBELLION AGAINST RUSSIA **35**

CHAPTER 5: THE CITY OF LIGHT............................**44**

CHAPTER 6: LOVE AND MUSIC IN PARIS............**58**

CHAPTER 7: CHOPIN AND SAND............................**69**

CHAPTER 8: THE DEATH AND LEGACY OF FREDERIC CHOPIN **84**

About KidCaps

KidLit-O is an imprint of BookCaps™ that is just for kids! Each month BookCaps will be releasing several books in this exciting imprint. Visit are website or like us on Facebook to see more!

To add your name to our mailing list, visit this link:
http://www.kidlito.com/mailing-list.html

Introduction

When you study famous musicians throughout history, a few big names come to mind: the famous Ludwig van Beethoven, who composed despite the fact that he grew deaf; Wolfgang Amadeus Mozart, who was an inspiration to all who came after him; Johann Sebastian Bach, who worked in many different places and met many different people. But there is one name that you will only see on occasion, and that is a man named Frederic Chopin.

Chopin, like many of his musical colleagues, was inspired by Mozart and all of the musicians that came before him. Most of his work was accomplished with the piano, which was created from the fortepiano and the organist in the decades before his birth. The work of Frederic Chopin helped build modern forms of classical music; he lived an exciting life and traveled many places and, if you wish to *truly* understand famous musicians, we must first understand the life of one whose influence is still felt today: Frederic Francois Chopin.

Chapter 1: Early Childhood

In the late 1700s, a man named Nicholas from France decided to travel to Poland. He wanted to live there and work as a bookkeeper. He moved to the Polish town of Zelazowa Wola. There, not only did he find a job as a bookkeeper, but he also became a teacher to the son of Warsaw's countess (the wife of the count that helped rule the city). It was here that Nicholas met a beautiful young woman named Tekla, who also worked in the count's estate. They instantly fell in love.

Nicholas and Tekla were married in 1806. Four years later, they had a baby boy that they decided to name Frederic. Frederic Chopin was born on March 1st, 1810 in the city of Zalazowa Wola. However, his parents did not think that they wanted stay in the city for very long.

They were not too happy working for the count, so they decided to move to the city of Warsaw, the capital of Poland. When the Chopins made the move, young Frederic was seven months old.

Nicholas was given some fantastic job opportunities in Warsaw. He was able to work at the Lyceum, which is a type of European school, and the Chopins lived in the Saxon Palace of Warsaw. It was definitely a better life than living in Zalazowa Wola! Nicholas was a teacher for many of the royal family members, called the *aristocracy*. This meant that he held a very important position. He was responsible for teaching the royal children everything they needed to know.

Living in Warsaw was great for young Frederic. He was able to see how life in a palace worked. He lived in a civilized area with very civilized people, and he had a proper and cultured upbringing. Some people think that this is the reason he became such a successful musician; others think his mother instilled it in him while still others think he just had the natural talent.

No matter what, however, his mother Tekla played a crucial role in Frederic Chopin's musical career. From the time he could walk and move his fingers, she was trying to teach him to play an instrument. By the time he was six years old, he could already play the music and writing his own music! Can you believe it?

Many scientists believe that childhood is the best time to learn an instrument. Because you are still young and your brain is learning all sorts of different things, you will have more time to tackle the piano and grow used to playing it. So, if you're thinking about playing the piano, do it as soon as possible!

His father and mother were stunned at how quickly he learned. They had never seen anything like it! They knew there was something special here, so they wanted to get Frederic the best teacher they could find, so his talent would not go to waste. They hired a man named Wojcheh Zywny, a famous musician in Warsaw.

Wojcheh was from the Czech Republic, a European country, and he taught Frederic for six years. Why did he stop? Well, Frederic soon became more talented than his teacher! Not even Wojcheh could believe it was true. People around Warsaw started to hear about the child prodigy Frederic Chopin. A *prodigy* is someone who is extremely talented at something; a very gifted singer might be called a prodigy, as well as an excellent cook. People called Frederic a prodigy at the piano.

They even said that he might become as talented as Wolfgang Amadeus Mozart and Ludwig van Beethoven, two of the most famous composers to ever walk the earth. Both of them had started playing instruments at an early age too, and also started writing music when they were young.

When Wojcheh began teaching Frederic, the young prodigy was already writing his own music. In fact, when he was seven, he wrote two songs that were immediately published because of how brilliant they were. Some people even believed that they were better than the leading songs of Warsaw's most popular musicians—and they were written by a seven-year-old child! The songs were called *polonaises*, which is a word for a Polish dance. Wojcheh helped Chopin understand classical music and how to officially write it, and we will talk more about classical music later. Like most people at the time, Wojcheh was listening to the works of Mozart and Beethoven, whom Chopin came to adore.

When people started talking about Chopin, the Polish government took notice. They all wanted to hear about the musical prodigy. They invited him to the Polish palaces to perform for them. This allowed him to spend more time around the Polish royalty, something that would give him great opportunities in life. As Frederic Chopin became more popular, he fell under the eye of one very important man.

His name was Grand Duke Constantine Pavlovich, and he ruled all of Poland. However, his brother ruled an even larger country: Russia. His brother's name was Alexander, and he ruled Russia as Tsar Alexander the First. *Tsar* is a term that was used for a Russian king; it is not used anymore.

Tsar Alexander the First came to visit his brother Constantine in Warsaw, and they all wanted to hear the seven-year- old musician play. As you can probably imagine, this was daunting for young Frederic! He was suddenly expected to play for two of the most powerful men in the world. But there was another level to this relationship between Poland and Russia that had been very disturbing for many people.

For years now, Poland had been living under Russian rule. Since Constantine and Alexander were brothers, Constantine allowed the tsar to rule his country — but this was *not* what the Polish people wanted. They wanted to be left alone. They wanted their independence. And because their Grand Duke did not give them that, they hated him. Frederic Chopin felt a little torn. On one hand, he was playing for royalty and he was becoming more famous every day. On the other hand, not many Polish people actually liked Constantine and Alexander.

The performance went spectacularly, however, and both the Grand Duke and the Tsar of Russia were very pleased with Frederic Chopin.

When Frederic was thirteen years old, his parents Nicholas and Tekla told him that he must study in the Lyceum of Warsaw. He took classes in music, math, Greek, and Latin. Learning both Greek and Latin was standard in the 1800s; almost every student was required to learn the languages, as they were seen as popular and necessary if you wanted to live in society.

In both of his musical and nonmusical studies, Frederic Chopin was excelling. His name was spreading like wildfire across Warsaw, across Poland, and across Europe.

Chapter 2: Rise of the Musical Prodigy

When Chopin first performed for Tsar Alexander the First, he did not know that he would see the tsar again. When Chopin was fifteen, the tsar visited Warsaw for a second time, and requested to hear a performance by the famous Frederic Chopin. Tsar Alexander the First even gave Chopin a gold ring as payment for his wonderful performances. Imagine being fifteen and already being a celebrity, called upon by one of the most feared men in the eastern hemisphere.

It was during this time that Chopin was composing one of his most famous pieces. It was called *Rondo in C minor, op.1*. *Rondo* is an Italian word that means a song with a theme that you hear over and over again. This theme will usually be found at the end of a piece, and that piece will typically be a concerto or even a sonata. *C minor* is just a way of telling people the *key* that the song is in; a song's *key* tells you what notes to play, much a like a key on a map tells you what to look for.

You can listen to the song online, and it is really quite beautiful! The song features the piano, since that was Frederic Chopin's main instrument. To think that a fifteen-year old wrote such a lovely piece is astonishing, and it gives you a great insight into how talented he truly was. When an author writes a book, he or she must think about every word they write; in the same way, a musician thinks hard and long about every note they put onto the page. Some of the piano usually plays more than one, two, or even three notes at once! *Rondo in C minor* lasts about eight minutes; it must have taken a lot of hard work for Chopin to write it!

Today, *Rondo in C minor* is not that popular, and many people tend to listen to and play some of his other songs. However, at the time, the rondo was revered by people everywhere. It was one of his most successful songs at the time.

His parents decided that Chopin's studies at the Lyceum would no longer do, and he needed to be moved to a new school that could accommodate his talent. So he decided to take classes at the Warsaw Conservatory, another very popular and renowned school.

At the Warsaw Conservatory, Chopin met a man by the name of Joseph Elsner. There, Elsner helped Chopin learn how to write even more advanced music, and also write music for different types of ensembles. Sure, Chopin knew how to write piano music for himself. But he was not great at writing music for larger orchestras and chamber groups. Chopin did not like writing for such big groups; he much preferred being limited to a single piano.

Elsner, of course, realized how skilled Chopin was. As a master piano teacher, even he was amazed at how well Chopin could play. He became one of the thousands who knew that there was something very special about Frederic Chopin. However, Elsner was one of the few people who knew *why* Chopin was so special: he did not only create music, he created *new* music.

This is the mark of famous musicians throughout history. They like to experiment with different techniques and forms of music, to put things down on the page in a certain order that no one had ever seen before. This is one of the reasons that Bach, Beethoven, and Mozart rose to celebrity status so quickly, and the same rule applies to Chopin.

Chopin liked to break the rules. When people told him that some part of his music was unusual or strange, he did not care. While most people revered Chopin for his brilliance and his experiments, some questioned him. When people asked Elsner why Chopin had a tendency to break the rules, Elsner replied, "Leave him in peace. his is an extraordinary path, for he has an extraordinary gift. He does not follow the old rules because he seeks those of his own."

As great as Chopin was at the piano, many historians and musical scholars believe that, while he did indeed have at least two teachers during his lifetime, most of his skills were self-taught. It seems he was just that talented. As a musician, Chopin loved to figure things out on his own and work with the piano. Music takes time to write, and he loved doing it.

During the rise of Frederic Chopin, his home life was mostly uneventful. He had three sisters: Ludwika, Emilia, and Izabela. The Chopin household was a musical one. While Chopin hammered away at the piano, so too did his mother Tekla; his father Nicholas was both a flute and a violin player (it's no wonder he grew up to be a musician, with so many musicians in the house!).

When he was seventeen years old, he suffered a terrible tragedy. His fourteen-year old sister Emilia died of *tuberculosis*. This is an infection of the lungs involving bacteria, and it was very prevalent in society until the mid-1900s. While it is no longer an enormous problem, thousands upon thousands of people contracted the disease in earlier centuries.

These made Frederic Chopin worried, because he himself had started to feel a little sick lately. He was always getting colds and had problems breathing, and he feared that he might get tuberculosis too. It is safe to say that he was sad and worried during this time in his life and, when you study a musician, it is very important to see what music they were writing during certain parts of their life, because you can often find connections.

While Chopin was sad, for instance, we know that he wrote the song *Nocturne in E minor*, with *E minor* once again just being an instruction on what notes to play. Anytime a song is mentioned here, you should definitely look it up and listen to it online. It will give you a much better idea of what the music sounds like, and maybe you can even understand what Chopin was feeling at the time.

Nocturne in E minor is a slow and sad song, and this makes perfect sense. While it is an absolutely beautiful piece of work, it unfortunately was never published during his lifetime. Only after his death was it revealed to the public, and audiences everywhere were astonished at how emotional and lovely the piece was. Today, this is one of the most popular Chopin pieces out there. For some people, it is relaxing and great music to unwind to; for others, it is a standard of the classical music era.

In the very next year, Frederic Chopin had the honor of meeting a man named Johann Nepomuk Hummel, a popular pianist was traveling to show off his talent. When he stopped in Warsaw to play for people, Chopin knew that he just *had* to go and see Hummel.

Hummel was older, around fifty years old, and of course he had heard of the musical prodigy who had been famous for over ten years now. He knew that he and Chopin would get along well, and indeed they did.

After talking with Hummel about tours, Chopin came to wonder about where he would go in his own life. He started to feel that maybe Warsaw was a bit too small. Not many famous musicians lived in Warsaw. He knew that he would need to travel if he wanted to expand his knowledge and meet other prodigies in the world of music. He thanked Johann Nepomuk Hummel, and made a plan.

The same year, in the month of September, Frederic Chopin traveled to Berlin, the capital of Germany. The distance between the two cities is 355 miles, and if we were to drive to Berlin by car, it would take us at least six hours. Poland and Germany are neighbors, however, so it could have taken a lot longer.

In Berlin, there were so many musical performances that Chopin hardly knew what to do with himself. While he liked going to orchestral performances, he *loved* listening to the opera. It was here that he started listening to opera often, and he continued to do so for the rest of his life. His trip to Berlin made a lasting impression on him, and he was very disappointed when he had to return to Warsaw.

In the year 1829, when Chopin was nineteen years old, another famous musician came to visit Warsaw, Poland. His name was Niccolo Paganini and he was a violinist extraordinaire. Chopin was not only a fan of Paganini's incredible talent, but also of his innovations. As we learned, a lot of famous musicians became so popular because they liked to experiment: Niccolo Paganini is a fantastic example of this, and he is one of the reasons that Chopin continued to write new and unusual music.

In fact, Paganini inspired Chopin to write a series of *etudes*. The word *etudes* is French for *studies*, and they are used as practice pieces. In an *etude*, a pianist will practice their technical skills—how fast they can move their fingers, how many notes they can reach with one hand, and so on. Typically, *etudes* are tedious and not that fun to play, especially when compared to great songs. However, Chopin wanted to change this. He wanted to write *etudes* that were not structured and boring, but were also artistic.

He succeeded. Chopin's *etudes* have been called some of the most successful pieces of music that combine technique with creativity. You can also find these online. They are a great listen, and can be used by any student attempting to learn the piano. If you want to learn the piano, it would be wise to use exercises created by one of the greatest piano players ever to exist!

But even though Frederic Chopin was invigorated by writing these excellent pieces of music, he wanted to leave Warsaw again. His memories of Berlin filled him with wonder. He knew that he needed to see the world—but this time, he would not travel to Berlin. He had another city in mind: Vienna, the capital of Austria.

Before he left for his trip, however, he had other thoughts on his mind.

Chapter 3: Chopin, the Romantic

Chopin came to realize that he was madly in love with one of his friends. Her name was Konstancya Gladkowska, and she was an absolutely lovely woman. She lived in the Warsaw Conservatory and she was a singer herself—and in Vienna, Chopin had come to adore vocal performances. He knew that he *had* to write a song about her—a song that would eventually become his *F Minor Concerto*. He was a nervous man, and always got cold feet around her. He decided that he would much rather show his affections for her through his music than through his words.

It took a long while before Chopin finally built up the courage to speak to her. He had hoped for the longest time that she would recognize him because of his music—which was not very hard, considering that people were raving about Chopin's songs from Warsaw, Poland to Moscow, Russia.

The two of them hit it off right away. Konstancya's dream was to be an opera singer, and she loved hearing Chopin talk about music—after all, he was very talented! And he loved hearing about her practicing and her performances. Chopin would often come to the Warsaw Conservatory so that he could see Konstancya. Sometimes, he would even play the piano in their classroom, while Konstancya and her best friend sang (the two of them were the star pupils in their chorus class).

But, as often happens when a famous artist grows to love someone, the feelings are easily spoiled with jealousy. Many different men visited Konstancya's class, two of them being Russian soldiers that served under the Grand Duke of Poland. The two men were clearly attempting to court Konstancya, and Frederic Chopin was insulted. He had not yet revealed to her his true feelings, and now he felt that he never would. He retreated into his room and started writing letters to his friend Titus.

Titus lived two hundred miles away, but Chopin still relied on him as one of his most trusted friends. Titus's advice was sound, and his logic was reasonable.

For someone like Chopin to experience this jealousy at the hand of two Russian soldiers just added insult to injury. Harsh feelings were still brewing about the Russian occupation of Poland. But Chopin was not the only aggravated one. It seemed like all of the Polish people were getting angrier, day by day. Even Frederic Chopin knew that something big was coming—but he did not know what.

Despite all of this, he continued talking with Konstancya, who had started taking vocal lessons with Henrietta Sontag, the greatest vocal singer of Chopin's time. He stopped by their practices and not only did he come to adore vocals even more, he became more infatuated with Konstancya. At this point, it was quite clear to Konstancya that Chopin had feelings for her. He spent all of time around her, he always asked to talk about her life—there was no doubt.

Chopin, however, did not think that he was loved back.

He would tell about how he planned to leave Warsaw soon. He had hoped that Konstancya would tell him how much she would miss him, or what she would do without him in Warsaw. She said nothing of the sort, however, which left Chopin feeling miserable.

Once again, during this time, Chopin wrote one of his most famous pieces. People everywhere have loved *F Minor Concerto,* and his new *E Minor Concerto* was even more of a hit. People were absolutely in love with his music. Never had songs for the piano been so vigorous and so easy to listen to. Chopin was changing the way that music was performed, one note at a time, and his audiences were thrilled to be along for the ride.

It was soon time for him to depart for Vienna, Austria, though. He wanted to give one final concert in Warsaw, what he would call a "Farewell Concert." Not only did he need to make money so that he could make the trip, but he wanted to say goodbye to the audiences that had been with him every step of the way—and he wanted to show off the music that he had written with Konstancya in his heart.

The concert was performed on October 11, 1830. He and Konstancya even performed together on stage; he played the piano while she sang. As you can imagine, the audiences fell in love with the two: Chopin, the most famous piano player in all of Europe, and Konstancya, an up-and-coming singer.

When the concert was over, Chopin was scheduled to depart. So what happened between him and Konstancya? Did they get together? Did he reveal his undying love for her? Well, that is one of the many mysteries of Frederic Chopin. Historians and scholars are not entirely sure what happened.

All we know is that Chopin convinced Konstancya to see him alone, and that no one knew what they were saying to each other. But whatever they said, Konstancya took one thing away from their meeting: a diamond wedding ring.

How did she feel about the ring? Did Chopin actually propose to her before he left? The world may never know. Chopin was closing one chapter in his life and opening another.

Chapter 4: Rebellion Against Russia

He left for Vienna when he was twenty years old. Why Vienna? Well, Vienna had long been a city of musical talent. Beethoven himself had traveled to Vienna so he could see Mozart, the musician Haydn spent time there, as well as a lesser-known, but influential, musician named Schubert.

He had expected to find people that he knew well there. For instance, he was friends with a man named Carl Czerny, a student who lived under Ludwig van Beethoven's instruction. He had expected to live among fellow musicians who all shared their talents and worked towards musical expertise. What he found, however, was quite a different environment.

In Vienna, everyone was competing for popularity. There were so many musicians in the city that Chopin hardly knew what to do. He faced harsh attitudes, something that was so different from the time he spent in Warsaw, where he was revered. In fact, Chopin ended up losing money over his trip to Vienna. He did not find many people interested in his music. He was a single fish lost in a very big school of fish.

His music came under criticism, something he had not experienced often. In Poland, people talked about how wonderful he was! Frederic Chopin, the man who had started writing music at seven years old. He wondered if he was more of a myth than an actual celebrity. His audiences said his playing was mediocre, that it was so small compared to the larger orchestras that were taking center stage. Beethoven himself wrote for larger ensembles than for single piano players, because that was what audiences wanted to hear. Bands were getting larger, music was getting louder, and some people did not have the patience to listen to a single quiet piano.

Chopin felt terribly lost.

His friend Titus had traveled with him to Vienna, however, which gave him some consolation. But after awhile in the city, Chopin and Titus were given some horrifying news.

The people of Poland had risen up in rebellion against the Russian government. The heart of the rebellion was in Warsaw, and shocking reports were coming out of the capital. Citizens were dead, soldiers were marching off to battle. Polish citizens were apparently calling everyone to arms, declaring that every man needed to rise up against the Russians. They wanted Polish independence, and they would do anything in their power to get it.

Immediately he wrote a letter to his family. He needed to see if they were okay. He knew that his family and friends were against the Russian government, and he also knew that if a fight broke out, they would rally to the freedom fighters, and that could get them killed. He told his family that he was going to leave Vienna right away and return home to Warsaw.

His family, though, did not think that was the greatest idea. They told him to remain safe in Vienna. As much as Chopin hated it, Titus told him he should listen to his family. It would be of no use for Chopin to rush to Warsaw and get himself killed.

But as much good advice as Titus gave, even he could not follow his own words. Titus soon told Chopin that he was leaving Vienna and going to fight the Russians in Warsaw. Chopin, justly, felt betrayed. How could Titus leave him alone in Austria? And why did Titus think it was okay to fight, but then opposed the idea of Chopin leaving?

Titus said that Chopin was far too weak to go and fight. After all, Chopin had been feeling sick and frail all these years. Could he really withstand battles against the ruthless Russian army? Even if he *was* too sick to go, Chopin was furious. All of his friends were going to fight for Polish independence, and he was stuck in Vienna, helpless.

But many scholars agree that Chopin was not truly helpless. As Titus pointed out, Chopin had a weapon that could be more dangerous than any sword or gun: music. He encouraged Chopin to write Polish music that would inspire the masses, which would convince them to rally to the aid of their country.

And so he continued to write music, but he was not happy about it. In fact, he was sad and tortured. All he could think about was Warsaw, his family, Titus, and of course, Konstancya. He followed every inkling of news about the Polish rebellion, praying his family and friends would come out of the fray alive.

At first, it seemed as if the Polish freedom fighters would succeed against the Russians, but this dream soon faded when the Russians won decisive victories in Warsaw. He was very happy to hear that his sisters, his mother, and his father had moved out of Warsaw and returned to Zelazowa Wola, where they could be safe. As for Konstancya, she and her family had also left the town. This took a great burden off of Chopin, but he still feared for the safety of the Polish people.

When we look at the music that Chopin was writing during this time, we can see a very drastic time. Whereas earlier his melodies had been very cheerful and easy to listen to, they were now dark and brooding. And who can blame him? His family and friends were thrown *into* danger, and he was countries away from them. Despite all of the distress that he felt, however, he knew that he needed to continue on.

There was no way he would be able to linger in Vienna for very long. Not only did people reject his music, they were not very nice to Polish people. He needed to leave—and fast—before something bad happened. He considered going to Italy for a time, but the country was facing a rebellion of its own. France would work just fine, he thought.

Paris, France would make a great home—after all, for decades it had been a center for art, science, and advanced thinking. It would be perfect, he thought, except he came across one small problem. He needed to travel through Poland in order to get to France—but the problem was not the Polish rebellion. In fact, he was going nowhere near the broken city of Warsaw.

When he tried to travel from Poland to France, he was told he would not be able to make it to Paris. This is because Poland was run by Russia, and Russia did not want many of its citizens leaving the country and going elsewhere. Suddenly, Chopin did not care how much Tsar Alexander had praised his music, or that the tsar had given him a gold ring.

Finally, the Russians allowed Chopin to depart for Paris.

He passed the gates of Paris in 1831, when he was twenty-one years old. He expected the city to be great, but he doubted it would ever be as popular as Vienna or Warsaw.

Chapter 5: The City of Light

No matter what he may have anticipated, Paris was completely different. It became like a second home to him! Compared to harsh Vienna, Paris was a lovely place. Music could be heard around every corner, the people were friendly (and *very* patriotic), and they also supported the Polish freedom fighters in their fight against Russia. By this point, the Russian soldiers had essentially crushed all hope of continued rebellion—but there were still those that whispered about the Polish people rising up once again.

Here is something that Beethoven said about Paris, in a letter to his friend Titus in Warsaw:

"It is the greatest splendor, the greatest vileness, the greatest virtue and greatest vice. Here is more noise, clamor, clatter, and dirt than can be imagined. One gets lost in this paradise, but lost comfortably, because no one cares how anyone else lives. One can walk in rags in the street and yet at the same time frequent the best company. One day you eat an abundant dinner for thirty-two [dollars] in a restaurant with mirrors, gold, and bright gas illumination, and the next day you may lunch at a place where they serve you portions fit for a bird and charge three times as much. . . . Paris is everything your heart desires—you may divert yourself, laugh, weep, do anything you please, and no one will pay any attention, for there are thousands doing the same thing as you, and each in his own way."

From this quotation, you can see that Chopin was infatuated with France. At the end he says that everyone was doing the same thing—but, unlike in Vienna, that did not mean that he faced much competition for musical superiority. In fact, the people of Paris adored Chopin and his music, and Chopin felt a greater sense of community—rather than contest—here.

He met many popular musicians, and he was honored to do so. After living in a lackluster musical community in Warsaw and experiencing a public disaster in Vienna, Paris was absolute heaven.

Here, a man by the name of Friedrich Kalkbrenner asked Chopin to be his student. He wanted to teach Chopin everything he knew—and Chopin would not have to pay a cent. So, what was the catch here? Well, Chopin wrote to his parents and asked for their advice. Why would one of the best musicians in Europe suddenly want to give Chopin lessons absolutely free? His parents thought that Kalkbrenner only wanted fame, so that he could say that *he* gave lessons to the famous Frederic Chopin.

Chopin did not listen to his parents, however. Nor did he listen to his fellow musicians, who told him that there was nothing Kalkbrenner could teach him that he did not already know. Everyone thought that Chopin was a far better piano player. Still, though, Chopin wanted to know what Kalkbrenner had to offer. After all, what did he have to lose by taking free lessons?

Time, apparently. Kalkbrenner quickly realized that there was nothing he could teach Chopin. In fact, Kalkbrenner ended up learning more from their intense lessons than Chopin did. What did Kalkbrenner expect when he took lessons from the most famous piano player in all of Europe?

And so the relationship between Chopin and Kalkbrenner did not last very long. Chopin was a god among men, and no one could rival his talent.

Throughout his time in Paris, he of course still despaired over the fate of his country. He especially missed Titus, who had been with him through thick and thin in Vienna. Now, Titus was gone, Poland defeated, and his heart was heavy. One day, he wrote to Titus:

"I wish that you were here. You won't believe how sad I am because I have no one to confide in. You know how easily I make friends, how I like to talk with them about nothing at all—and I have such friends, more than I can count, but no one with whom I can share my feelings. That's why I get tired, and you won't believe how much I crave some respite, a whole day when no one will be talking to me."

Even though Chopin was famous and was the life of the party in Paris, he felt lonely. He had friends, of course, but no close friends with whom he could share his feelings. And just when he thought things could not make him feel worse, of course they did.

His sister Isabella sent him a letter with sad news. Konstancya had recently married a man named Joseph Grabowski, someone that she had known for a great deal of her life. Chopin was offended and deeply saddened. Was this why she had never shown him any affection while he was in Warsaw? Because she had always loved another man? If that was so, then his songs for her were nothing, along with the wedding ring and all of the time he had spent thinking about her.

He was so upset by this that he never mentioned her again.

Just as his move to Vienna had begun a new chapter in his life, so too did this news close one chapter and open another. He was now free from thinking about her; no longer did he have to worry about her love, or how she had seemed so aloof when he was with her. Chopin would begin anew here.

Even for his Parisian audiences, though, Chopin faced some difficulties. Many people were not accustomed to his strange music. Some people thought it was because he was too young and that he would gain more experience and knowledge with time. But still Chopin could not understand why he was not gaining more of an audience. He had been praised and worshipped in Warsaw, but both Vienna and Paris were full of criticism. But where else could he go?

London, England? The United States of America? At the time, America had experienced a great influx of immigration, especially from Italians, the Irish, Poles, and Germans. People far and wide talked about America being the land of opportunity and freedom. Was this the reality? Well, not necessarily for foreigners. While many people flocked there to escape oppression and to get rich, many people only found low-paying jobs and expensive prices.

Still, though, the idea that America was the land of opportunity persisted in Europe. When he told people that he wanted to move there, they were shocked. Why would he travel so far? Would he even have the money to do so? Was he sure he would find the right supportive audiences in the United States? His parents were especially surprised to hear Chopin's notion of moving there. His father recommended that he moved back to Warsaw, now that much of the rebellion had calmed down. But Chopin flatly refused. Until the Poles had gained their independence, he did not want to walk among the streets of Warsaw.

Just as he was convinced that he would travel across the Atlantic Ocean and start a new life in America, he ran into someone of high esteem in Paris. The man's name was Prince Valentin Radziwill, who was related to a man named Antoni who lived in Warsaw. Antoni happened to be a *huge* fan of Frederic Chopin, admiring all of his music. When Prince Valentin found out that he was talking to Chopin, he was amazed!

But he did find Chopin in a happy state. Frederic Chopin was disappointed that he had to move from Paris and start over. The prince, however, simply would not hear it. How could Frederic Chopin not find a supportive audience in Paris, of all places? He told Chopin that they were both immediately going to the home of Baron James de Rothschild.

Baron de Rothschild was one of the richest men in Paris, and he had come from a long line of rich bankers. He loved art and music and literature, and he had of course heard Frederic Chopin's name. Chopin played for Baron de Rothschild and his family, and they were simply astounded at his talent and expertise.

Baroness de Rothschild asked if Chopin would give her lessons. She was a piano player herself and there was absolutely no one better in all of Paris to turn to. The Rothschild family spread word of Chopin, and convinced all of their wealthy friends that he was worth listening to. Calls began coming in the mail—rich families and politicians wanted Chopin to play for them, and he followed through with their requests.

He was happy, for he had a very sudden change of fortune when things seemed their absolute worst. He did not have to turn to extreme circumstances after all; Chopin would be okay. In a letter to one of his friends, Chopin wrote the following:

"I have entered the highest society. I sit among ambassadors, princes, and ministers, and I don't know by what miracle this came to pass, because I myself made no effort to get there. It is very important for me . . . the moment you have been heard at the English or Austrian embassy, they assume you have a great talent [. . . .] If I were more stupid than I am, I would think that I am at the peak of my career, but I realize how much remains to be done, and I realize it all the more because I am close to the foremost artists and I know what each of them is lacking. . . . If you haven't forgotten what I'm like, you will know that I am the same today as I was yesterday, with this difference—that I have one side whisker, while the other refuses to grow. I have to give five lessons today. You'd think I am making a fortune. But a carriage and white gloves, without which a man has no *bon ton*, cost more than I have. At heart I am a revolutionary—hence I care not at all for money, but only for friendship."

This is quite astounding to read. Frederic Chopin had never been truly poor in his life, but he still recognized his luck. He was completely grateful to the Baron de Rothschild for his help, and he still did not worship money. Lesser men might have been greedy, demanding high prices and becoming cruel to those below him. But Chopin was a kind man at heart, whose fortunes had reversed for the better.

Because the wealthy men and ladies of Paris started to adore Frederic Chopin, so too did everyone else. They wanted to follow suit. Chopin was becoming *really* popular now, so popular that he got his own publisher. His publisher would print his works, people would buy the sheet music so that they could play it, and then Chopin made money. Things had turned around for him.

Chapter 6: Love and Music in Paris

Chopin certainly was living an interesting life. By day, he gave at least five piano lessons. By night, he visited many of Paris's famous aristocrats, visiting ambassadors, and wealthy bankers. He was now living among royalty.

Ever since he found out that Konstancya had been engaged, Chopin had not thought too much about love, especially with his schedule filled up nearly every day. But as he visited Paris's royalty, he came across one woman whom he simply could not get out of his mind.

Her name was Countess Delphine Potocka. He had seen her several times, once even during his time in Germany. Now, though, he saw her numerous nights at the homes of many different aristocrats and bankers. He enjoyed her company. Their conversation flowed and was sprinkled with laughter. The two of them got along very well and, to Frederic Chopin's ecstatic delight, she was a singer. Chopin thought that she could have sung at any opera or concert across France, but she only laughed and said that that had never interested her. In fact, she liked to sing alone with a piano playing.

Chopin gave her some music lessons; he was not the best singer, but together he would play the piano and she would sing. Today, many music teachers use Chopin's methods for instruction. You will often see solo singers accompanied by a piano. Chopin perfected the art of putting these two instruments together, and influenced the way in which music would be performed in the future.

In addition to this, however, she wanted to learn to play the piano. He instructed her in that as well, and she was a very eager student. She hung onto his every word, for he was truly the master of the piano. For any student of music, or who wishes to know what his instruction was like, here was something he wrote for her:

"To an accomplished virtuoso all tricks are permitted. He should use his own methods by all means. You may put your thumb under your little finger, if it is an advantage in the execution of the passages. If necessary, take two white or even two black keys with one finger. If you put the third finger over the fourth or even the fifth, you won't be committing a mortal sin either. Don't tire the fourth finger too much; it is so close connected with the third that you'll never succeed in making it quite independent. My fourth finger is completely untrained, yet I can manage it in such a way that no one would notice. Each finger is built differently; each has a different strength and function. One mustn't destroy but on the contrary develop the subtlety of touch that is proper and natural to each finger.

"Play Bach's 'Preludes' and 'Fugues' every day. This is the best school; no one will ever create a better. If you have plenty of time, memorize Bach; only by memorizing a work does one become thoroughly acquitted with it. Without Bach you cannot have freedom in the fingers, nor a clear and beautiful tone. A pianist who doesn't recognize Bach is a fool.

"Bach will never become old. His works are written like those ideally conceived geometric figures in which everything is in its proper place and not a single line superfluous. . . . When I play another composer's work, I often think that I would have solved or written this or that passage in a different way. But when I play Bach, I never feel like this. Everything he does is perfect; it is not possible to imagine it otherwise, and the slightest change would spoil everything."

So, as you can see, Frederic Chopin was quite the fan of Johann Sebastian Bach. Why? Bach is one of the greatest musicians to ever live, because he experimented and created new music that people had never heard or thought of before. If you read the first lines of Chopin's letter again, you will see that he encourages Countess Potocka to break the rules. No piano player will be punished for experimenting with new notes and methods, and this is one of the reasons that Chopin remains so famous today.

Considering the amount of letters that were exchanged between Chopin and Countess Potocka, and the amount of time they spent together, we know that they were good friends. He composed much of his music with her in mind, and he loved playing the pieces in front of her.

The rise of classical music had given musicians a very special place in society. Before this era, most people just assumed that musicians were like servants. They were ordered to play songs, be paid, and go on their way. But with music becoming so popular, musicians were soon treated like celebrities. Ludwig van Beethoven was one of the first to be treated like this, with Frederic Chopin coming soon after.

As the years wore on, he wrote more music. He met more aristocrats, royalty, bankers and foreign ambassadors. He also began to hate playing in public. He did not like being around crowds so much and being the center of attention. Just as he preferred to write for just a few people, maybe a piano and a singer, he did not like playing for a large audience.

Over the summers, he would spend time with the Wodzinski family, a group of aristocrats who had fled Warsaw when the Polish rebellion broke out. Chopin had tutored Maria Wodzinski, and he had quickly become good friends with the family. Also one summer, he met up with his parents, who had not seen him in five years. They met in the city of Carlsbad and spent three weeks together.

As you can probably imagine, Chopin was thrilled to see them. They had been living in Warsaw again for awhile now. Since the rebellion had been crushed and the Russian troops calmed down, things had not been so bad. They asked Chopin to walk them back to Warsaw, but he refused. Like he had said, he would not step foot in the streets of Warsaw until the Russian regime had been overthrown and Polish independence restored. They said their farewells on the border of Poland. Little did Frederic Chopin know that this was the last time he would see his parents.

On his way back to Paris, he stayed with the Wodzinskis in the summer home in Dresden, Germany. He enjoyed spending time with them. They asked him about his time in Carlsbad with his parents; to Chopin, the Wodzinskis were like a second family, and he loved spending time with Maria.

Maria was incredibly intelligent and she loved to sing and play the piano— needless to say, she and Chopin got along incredibly well. Sometimes she would sing so that she could donate money to charity. Even if she was not the prettiest girl in Paris, people loved her for her attitude and her talent.

Back in Paris, he started to think that the two of them might make a lovely couple. He exchanged some letters with her, some of which hinted that she missed him and enjoyed it when he visited. Countess Potocka was no longer an option for his affections, since she had suddenly departed Paris.

Chopin, who was afraid of being rejected and alone after his experiences with Konstancya, needed someone to turn to; Maria Wodzinski was the first person on his list, as a great and trusted friend. He came to love her so much that he intended to propose to her and ask for her hand in marriage. He sent a letter to his parents about his plan, and they were very happy with it. They thought Maria was a lovely girl, and the fact that her family was absolutely rich certainly played a role in the decision.

It took quite awhile for him to ask her, though. For one, Chopin kept on falling dangerously sick—so ill, in fact, that some people in Warsaw whispered rumors that he had died. It was not true, of course, but Chopin's health was obviously failing and the early death of his sister lingered in his mind. He knew that he needed to propose to Maria, and soon.

Before he did so, however, he needed to get permission from Maria's mother and father. When he asked the mother, she immediately gave her consent. She thought it was a lovely idea! But as he was about to ask Maria's father, he got cold feet. How was he, the son of a poor schoolteacher, supposed to live up the expectations of the wealthy aristocrats? Many people think that, if Chopin asked, Maria would have said yes. No matter Chopin's social class or his origins, he was well-liked and was revolutionizing the world of music.

Very slowly, Chopin and Maria grew distant. They barely saw each other, and their letters were brief and meaningless. Chopin had missed a grand opportunity to marry a wonderful woman.

Chapter 7: Chopin and Sand

Despite the sorrow that Chopin felt in his heart, though, life went on. Chopin spent less time performing and more time in his home, working on music and inviting guests to listen to him. Especially with his worsening his health, this is how he wished to spend the later years of his life.

On one night in particular, Chopin invited a popular French author by the name of George Sand—but George Sand was not necessarily who "he" claimed to be.

George Sand was a woman, actually named Aurore Dupin. She did not believe that many people would read her literature if they knew she was a woman, since men tended to dominate society unfairly. Even in modern days, we can see examples of this. When J.K. Rowling released *Harry Potter and the Sorcerer's Stone*, she used her first initials "J.K." because she thought people might not take her seriously if they knew it was written by a woman.

"George Sand" spent most of her nights in the high circles of Parisian life, floating from house to house. Chopin found her particularly interesting and beautiful—in fact, he once compared her looks to those of Maria.

Sand did not like to join in on conversation, but rather sit by the fire and smoke. Chopin was intimidated by her casualness and her strangeness. Something drew him to her though. He saw her every now and then, most often in the house of Lizst, another famous musician who lived in Paris. Slowly the two of them became friends. It was certainly one of Chopin's more interesting friendships, since Sand was so eccentric.

The two of them were artistic geniuses, despite working in very different fields. For one, they were from different countries. While Chopin was a Polish nationalist, meaning he was very patriotic in his country, Sand was French, and deep inside he wanted to marry someone who was Polish. He hammered away at his music until it was perfect; she sent her manuscripts immediately to the publishers without taking a second glance at them. He spent most of his time among the wealthy aristocrats; she spent most of her time living with artists who spat upon the idea of extraordinary wealth.

Despite their differences, the two of them became very good friends. At the same time that Frederic Chopin was becoming horribly ill, even at the age of twenty-seven, Sand's son Maurice was sick as well in Italy. She knew that she needed to go and visit her son, but she wanted Chopin to come along. Could he really travel so far in his sick condition?

He decided to travel with her no matter his health. He thought that the warmer weather in Italy might be good for him, and from what we can tell in his letters, he certainly liked the weather in Italy. See this quotation from Frederic's pen:

"I am in Palma, along palms, cedars, cacti, olives, oranges, lemons, figs, pomegranates, etc.—everything that the Jardin des Plantes has in its hothouses. The sky is like turquoise, the sea like lapis lazuli, the mountains emerald, the air is heavenly. Sun all day, everyone wears summer clothes, it is hot; at night, guitars and singing for hours on end. Enormous balconies with grapevines overhead. Moorish walls. Everything turns its face toward Africa, as the whole town does. In a word, a marvelous life."

The experience of Italy certainly did not put a damper on Chopin; even with his growing ailment, he found joy in the warm country and the company of Sand. Occasionally, Chopin would go out and walk around the towering mountains. He found the people, the culture, and the land so different than in Poland or France. It was fascinating!

But something happened that he did not expect. One day, as he was walking among the mountains, a terrible storm struck and Chopin was caught in the rain. He rushed back to Sand, a distance of three miles. His clothes had soaked through and he was coughing miserably. He caught a cold instantly, and it was not pretty.

Sand quickly called three of the best doctors in the local town, and they all said that he had bronchitis, a sickness in the lungs. It causes rampant coughing and chest pain. Needless to say, Chopin was in extreme discomfort, but he had Sand there, who was willing to take care of him every step of the way.

The sickness made it difficult for Chopin to focus on his music. Because of this, and because it was worsening, news spread quickly. People started to worry for Chopin and for his music. Not everyone was sympathetic. Some people believed, and some believe today, that Chopin also suffered from tuberculosis, which is contagious. Chopin and Sand were chased out of their house and their town. Tuberculosis (or TB for short) was much feared; the townspeople did not care *who* Chopin was, they would not have him put all of their lives at risk.

Where were they to go? They decided to stay in a monastery in the side of a mountain. A monastery is a place where monks live, and a place where travelers could often stay for refuge from weather. However, there were no monks at this place. Only three people still lived in the lonely monastery: a gatekeeper, a cook, and a pharmacist. Even though it was mostly abandoned, it was kept in great shape and was beautiful.

Frederic Chopin left us details of what the monastery looked like, and what he thought of it:

"My cell has the shape of a tall coffin. The enormous vaulting is covered with dust; the window is small. Outside the window there are orange trees, palms, and cypresses. Opposite the window stands my bed under a Moorish filigree rosette. Next to the bed there is an old square writing desk that I can scarcely use; on it a leaden candle stick (this is a great luxury here) with a candle. Bach, my scribblings, and old papers (not mine)—silence. One can yell . . . still silence."

For one studying the life of Chopin, it is amazing to see that he traveled so far. For someone who had been dining amongst the highest Parisian royalty not too long ago, here he was in an abandoned monastery. The winter did not bring him any comfort, either. The rain and snowstorms were harsh, and they threatened Chopin's health.

When the winter had ended, however, he decided it might be best for him to return to France. Both Sand and her son Maurice came with him. For Chopin, the monastery was just too quiet and haunting. Every night, one of the men who still lived there would come banging on the doors, shouting the names of every monk who had left. He would then fall asleep in the middle of the hall, with a knife in one hand and a rosary in the other. It was indeed time for Chopin to return to Paris.

They did not go directly to the capital. Instead, they stayed at a house that Sand owned in the town of Nohant. It was situated in the center of France, in the middle of the woods. It was quite cozy, and Chopin certainly came to adore the place. Sand took the best care of Chopin, constantly checking on his health and making sure he was as comfortable as he could be.

When the three of them finally returned to Paris, Chopin was shocked to find that someone from his past had turned up in the city: Countess Delphine Potocka. It is talked about very little, but it must be understood that Chopin had never truly forgotten about her, and had even harbored romantic feelings for her all of his life. She was one of his closest friends, even if they had not talked as often as he would have liked.

He wrote a letter to Countess Potocka, concerning his relationship with Sand and his affections:

"Only you and Sand have had my heart, and you more than anyone else because you know and understand me as no one else does. I haven't opened my heart to her; she is a foreigner and would not understand me."

This may seem surprising to a lot of people. It seems like Sand would have been the best partner for Chopin, considering how carefully and diligently she took care of him. But there was one thing about Chopin that made up his mind: he was a Polish patriot, and Sand was too French for him. This may seem silly to us today, but for Chopin it was sadly a deciding factor.

Did he ever truly love Sand, though? Or did he just decide that he could never marry her? The world may never know. He never did dedicate a piece to George Sand, although he had dedicated several to Countess Potocka.

Around this time in Paris, Chopin received the sad news that his father had passed away at the age of seventy-two. Once again, this made Chopin feel nervous about his own health. His bronchitis and possible tuberculosis was only getting worse, and it made him worried about his future. As if to make things worse, arguments between George Sand and Chopin forced Sand and her son to move away.

They still saw each other on occasion, but their relationship could not be what it once was. Against this romantic backdrop, Chopin suffered another blow to the heart. The Polish people had started to rise again, in what would become known as the Revolution 1848. The revolution occurred in many European countries, but Chopin really only cared about Poland.

Polish citizens living in Paris flocked to Warsaw to fight the Russian regime. Many of the Parisians supported the Polish cause, as they themselves had experienced much oppression in their history. Chopin's health was too poor, however. There was no way he would be able to make it to Warsaw, much less fight in a revolution. And there were venues for music in Paris now, as most of the city's attention was on the mass Revolution against oppressive governments. Because of this Chopin decided that he must leave Paris, and go to London, England.

London, however, was probably not the best idea. A city known for its rainy and cold climate, London would do nothing to help Chopin's worsening health. Upon the advice of a doctor, Chopin returned to Paris once again, where he came to a startling realization: he did not have much longer to live. He could feel death slowly closing in on him. He told his remaining family just how bad he was getting, which he had hid from them for some time.

Chapter 8: The Death and Legacy of Frederic Chopin

Countess Delphine Potocka heard that Chopin was near death and she traveled directly to him. When she arrived, Chopin said some memorable words that reveal his true feelings for her:

"It was to enable me to see you that God has postponed calling me to him."

In his final hours, Chopin asked Potocka to sing for him. He had always liked hearing vocals, and Potocka had such a sweet beautiful voice. She sang two songs, "Hymn to the Virgin" and "Psalm." It was difficult for her to sing at a time like this, when all she wanted to do was cry for the dying musician.

Chopin died two days later in the middle of the night, at the age of thirty-nine. People across the globe were devastated.

The famous musician's works had reached America and gone even into Asia. Everyone revered Chopin as one of the most creative and innovative piano players of the time. It is very easy to underestimate Frederic Chopin in terms of classical music. After all, he rarely wrote for vocals, and even more rarely wrote for strings or horns. The piano was his sole instrument.

Chopin let the world know that you not need "rules" to play the piano. You could play however you wanted to play, so long as you were making your own music. Like the famous composers that came before him, Chopin was a fan of breaking traditions and experimenting with music. Much of his music was of a style that had never seen before; it required incredible technique on one hand, and extensive creativity on the other.

If you ever play the piano, chances are you will come into contact with some of Chopin's work, whether it is a basic exercise or one of his more advanced concertos. Sure, he may not have written for huge orchestras, but he changed the way that the world looked at the piano, and also the way that the world respected musicians.

Frederic Chopin is a musician whose innovations will last for as long as pianos continue to play music.